Woe Be Th
Ever Asks His Wife
To Hustle and
Other
Tales of Woe

For Bertie & Dan.
This was fun to write.
Linda is involved in all except
the first chapter.
Enjoy!
Harb (Howard)

Howard Henry

Copyright © 2023 by Howard Henry

All rights reserved.

No portion of this book may be reproduced in any form without written permission from the publisher or author, except as permitted by U.S. copyright law.

DEDICATION

This book is dedicated to my late wife Linda. She was the inspiration (not intentionally) for the book. While it may seem that she was frequently upset, that was not the case at all. We had a great, loving, long marriage.

FORWARD

This book is based on actual experiences of the author primarily with his wife. It could easily be between any couple where one causes or receives and one administers or shares the woe. Woe is almost always involved in sporting events, almost any medical issue and with automobiles. That would have been too easy—this is looking at the aspect of the relationship between a couple.

Contents

Dedication i
Forward ii
Introduction 1
Chapter 1 Who Does Not Heed a Barking Dog 2
Chapter 2 Who Ever Has Two Dates Scheduled at the Same Time 6
Chapter 3 Who Never Takes His Wife on a Scheduled Honeymoon 12
Chapter 4 Doesn't Think Through The First Few Days Of Marriage. 16
Chapter 5 Who is Not Prepared for the Sharing of Woe 21
Chapter 6 Who Does Not Take it Easy at the Christmas Party 26
Chapter 7 Who Thinks He Can Go Jogging 32
Chapter 8 Who Ever Asks His Wife to Hustle 38
Chapter 9 Who Is Not Aware of His Wife's Real Shopping Plan 42
Chapter 10 Who Is Not Prepared for the Transfer of Woe 46
Chapter 11 Who Tries to Use Logic with His Wife 50
Chapter 12 Who Thinks He is Lost 54
Chapter 13 Who Ever Has to Shop for a Bra for His Wife 59
Chapter 14 Who Ever Suggests His Wife Needs to get Her Hearing Checked
.... 63
Chapter 15 Who is Not Prepared for His Wife's Weight Gain 67
Chapter 16 Who is Not Prepared for the "Event" 72
Conclusion 77

INTRODUCTION

Woe has many meanings. At the start of each chapter is a listing of some of them for easy reference. Following that are a couple of paragraphs explaining how woe can often be conveyed like "the look" or "the silent treatment".

Most of the woe incurred by a husband is self-inflected—something that could have been avoided if the husband thought through what he was doing. The next area is inflected woe be it something unavoidable or purposely done by his wife. Sometimes that done by his wife comes under the heading of "sharing woe" or the "transfer of woe".

One other woe is considered to be inevitable—one that is going to happen in life and there is nothing you can do to avoid it.

All of the above are noted in the chapters following and are between a husband (the author) and his wife. The first chapter involves a girlfriend before marriage but still is between a man and a woman. The second chapter is also before marriage and you will see the relationships there. Hopefully this book will bring a smile to your face from time to time.

CHAPTER 1

WHO DOES NOT HEED A BARKING DOG

Woe is a word that has been around for a long time. It appears at least 100 times in the Bible. Some of the many definitions of the word are misery, suffering, trouble, pain, disaster, depression, distress, grief, agony, gloom, sadness, hardship, sorrow, anguish, misfortune, unhappiness, heartache, heartbreak, adversity, dejection, wretchedness.

However, there can be additional circumstances that a husband or boyfriend can experience that go along with the above. One such example is what I call "the look" which is a piercing, hard glare that conveys much of the above and the man now understands that something is amiss and more woe will follow. Another tactic employed by some women is the silent treatment which can last for days on end. It is a powerful tool that can create loneliness and leave the man wondering what he did wrong and when will it ever end.

Then there are insidious tactics— like maneuvers that seem innocent enough but put a man in a vulnerable position. Some could be called external involving the transferring or sharing of woe. It should be noted that most of the woe incurred by a man is what would be called self-inflicted where even a small misstep can lead to monumental amounts of woe. This episode will address an inflicted woe.

Once upon a time, when I was just a young lad in high school, I mustered up the courage to ask a fair maiden named Edith out on a date. Little did I know this date would turn out to be a woeful adventure. Edith resided on a charming farm a few miles outside of town. As I pulled up to her estate, I found myself on a winding dirt road leading to a gate. It was at this point that I had to exit my vehicle and open the gate to continue my journey towards Edith's abode, nestled in the countryside just beyond. As I got out of the car I could hear a dog barking in the distance. Little did I know that this would later become a symbol of my misfortune.

On a pleasant evening, I took Edith out for a delightful time at the movies and later to the drive-in for some snacks. As the night grew on, I knew it was time to take her home, so we made our way back to her farm. Upon arriving, I had to unlatch the gate once more, but she assured me it would be safe to leave it open since the cows were tucked away by their barn for the night. As we stepped out of the car, a distant dog's barking caught my attention, but I didn't give it much thought.

We talked a bit while on her front porch, and as I was preparing to kiss her goodnight, I caught a blur in my eye. A massively large black dog without a sound was headed right for us! As I turned toward the dog, a large amount of woe latched onto my leg with great snarling. Shock and pain, and fear were instantly inflicted. Edith grabbed the dog's collar and pulled him back. Her next words were, "You probably ought to go." Without hesitation, I "hustled" (note that from another episode) very quickly to the car.

As I sped toward the gate, I remembered it was open and stopped to close it, hoping that Edith had the dog. Unfortunately, the dog had followed me and was now snarling at the car. I was able to get the door shut just as he got there and floored the accelerator racing back to the main road. Brutus or Killer or whatever his name was gave up eventually. It took some time for my heart to return to normal. When I got home, I was relieved to find that my jeans prevented any serious injury.

Somehow, I never managed to ask Edith out again. One never knows what could have developed in that relationship. It certainly would not have included her dog. Woe can take many forms and this was not one to be repeated.

CHAPTER 2

WHO EVER HAS TWO DATES SCHEDULED AT THE SAME TIME

Woe is a word that has been around for a long time. It appears over 100 times in the Bible. Some of the many definitions of the word are: "misery, suffering, trouble, pain, disaster, depression, distress, grief, agony, gloom, sadness, hardship, sorrow, anguish, misfortune, unhappiness, heartache, heartbreak, adversity, dejection, wretchedness".

However, there can be additional circumstances that a husband or boyfriend can experience with their significant other that go along with the above. Open communication can resolve some of these conflicts—others take a subtler yet intense form.

One such example is what I call "the look," which is a piercing, hard glare that conveys much of the above, and the man now understands that something is amiss and more woe will follow. Another tactic employed by some women is the silent treatment which can last for days on end. It is a powerful tool that can create loneliness and leave the man wondering what he did wrong and when it will ever end.

Then there are insidious tactics—like maneuvers that seem innocent enough but put a man in a vulnerable position. Some could be called external, involving the transferring or sharing of woe. It should be noted that most of the woe incurred by a man is what would be called self-inflicted, where even a small misstep can lead to monumental amounts of woe. This episode will address a self-inflicted woe.

As a man reflects upon courtship rituals, he cannot help but recall the countless occasions in which he found himself racking his brain to conjure up the perfect date. Oh, the trials and tribulations of it all! Yet, let me be clear, my aim today is not to recount the arduous task of devising a date. No, rather, I wish to share with you an experience that I endured, an experience that no man should ever have to face. You see, I had a steady girlfriend, but what unfolded on that fateful day was a journey no man will ever forget.

As I reminisce on my younger years, one particular summer comes to mind. I was a college student with a summer job in south central Missouri, and my beloved girlfriend resided in the bustling city of St. Louis. As I recall, that summer, it was the typical hot, humid Missouri that one would expect. I looked forward to a nice weekend with my steady. Despite the distance between us, we made it a priority to see each other about every weekend. However, on that fateful weekend, my heart sank as my love informed me that she had plans with her girlfriends and would not be making the long journey to see me. Although I attempted to conceal my disappointment, I mustered up the courage to assure her that I would be fine and that we could plan to reunite the following weekend. Ah, if only I knew the events that would unfold in the coming days.

In the meantime, there was this beautiful girl in the next town that I had just met who was visiting her folks, and because I knew I was free for the weekend, I asked her out for a Friday night. She mentioned that she had been seeing another guy, but that was where she worked in Kansas, some 250 miles away, and we both agreed that a night out together would be fun. So, this seemed to be a perfect situation.

Now it happened that my two sisters were home about that time and learned I would have a date with someone other than my steady. Of course, there were a few comments, mainly in a negative way (being true, etc.). However, I was looking forward to the evening as any young man would for a date with a good-looking female. We planned on going to a night spot in another town with a band, and we could dance into the evening.

Then one of the worst things that could happen came true as I trudged home after a long day at work, I had no inkling of the dreadful news that awaited me. It was a time before the advent of cell phones, and so I was caught off guard when my sister informed me that my beloved girlfriend had called with a change of heart and was en-route to my humble abode. The clock struck at 5:15 pm, and my heart sank as I contemplated the imminent arrival of my love. She would be here about the same time I would need to pick up my intended date! I was aghast, to say the least. The sheer weight of the situation was enough to make me break out into a cold sweat. The words "what am I going to do?" echoed in my head as I wrung my hands in despair, my poor wretched body consumed by a feeling of utter hopelessness.

As if the weight of the world was not enough, my two sisters descended upon me with great gusto, their words cutting like a thousand knives. With an almost gleeful tone, they bombarded me with jabs like, "So, how are you going to get out of this one, huh?" and "Way to go, Romeo!" Their words were like daggers, each one plunging deeper into my already shattered soul. Even my dear mother seemed to have conveniently found other tasks to occupy herself with, a sly smile playing on her lips as if amused by my plight. The woe that had engulfed me seemed to worsen with every passing moment, like a heavy fog that refused to dissipate, leaving me to flounder in its depths for what felt like an eternity.

In a twist of fate that seemed almost too miraculous to be believed, something truly incredible occurred. In the midst of my despair, I resigned myself to the fact that I would have to cancel my plans with a beautiful girl from a neighboring town, my heart heavy with regret. As I slowly made my way towards the phone, bracing myself for the inevitable disappointment, it suddenly rang. With trembling hands, I picked up the receiver, unsure of what to expect on the other end. And there she was — the very girl I was about to call, her voice like music to my ears. She was calling me to tell me that she needed to break our date because she had received a call from her boyfriend, and he was on his way to meet her parents.

It was as if the heavens had parted, and a ray of hope had shone down on me in that moment of darkness. Her voice was like a cool breeze on a scorching summer day, a balm to my frayed nerves. It was as if she had sensed my distress and had reached out to me just in the nick of time. At that moment, all of the worry and despair that had weighed heavily on my mind lifted, replaced by a newfound sense of hope and optimism. The world suddenly seemed brighter, the colors more vivid, as if the very air around me had been charged with a renewed sense of purpose. I couldn't believe my luck — *it was as if fate had intervened, providing me with a lifeline when I needed it most. At that moment, I knew that everything was going to be alright.*

As she spoke those words of apology, I felt a pang of disappointment. But I couldn't help but admire her honesty and sincerity — it was a rare quality in a world where people often said one thing and meant another. I reassured her that it was perfectly alright, hiding my own disappointment behind a facade of politeness. I wished her and her boyfriend all the best, my voice laced with a tinge of envy. In truth, I was glad that I had been spared the awkwardness of having to cancel a date myself.

But as soon as I hung up the phone, a surge of relief washed over me. It was as if a weight had been lifted from my shoulders, and I could finally breathe easily again. I realized that I had been spared a potentially disastrous situation and that the universe had aligned in my favor. I was grateful for this stroke of luck, and I couldn't help but smile to myself, marveling at the whims of fate.

As I reveled in my good fortune, I couldn't help but notice the scowls on my sisters' faces. Their once-cheery expressions had transformed into a mix of envy and annoyance, and their eyes seemed to bore into my very soul. It was clear that they were not happy about my sudden stroke of luck, and I couldn't help but feel a twinge of guilt mixed in with my happiness. But at that moment, nothing could dampen my spirits.

As I reflect back on that fateful day, I can't help but wonder if fate had intervened or if my mischievous sisters had a hand in the events that unfolded. Did they conspire with my girlfriend to arrange her unexpected return home and then gleefully watch as I writhed in woe? The truth may never be known.

I never told my girlfriend, who became my wife for many years about this fateful day. And I never heard if the other girl who married her boyfriend ever told him.

I can't help but wonder if my wife would have found the same humor in it as I do. Would she have laughed at my moment of woe and the improbable twist of fate that saved me? Or would she scold me for my naivete and my sisters' mischief?

As with most stories of woe and triumph, there are lessons to be learned. And in this case, the lessons were clear as day. Firstly, don't let your sisters in on your plans, for they can be mischievous creatures who take pleasure in causing distress. But more importantly, stay true to the one you love, and don't let the siren call of a pretty face lead you astray.

Of course, hindsight is always 20/20, and in the heat of the moment, rationality tends to fly out the window. But in the end, it all worked out for the best. Fate, it seems, had a way of intervening and setting things right. And though there were moments of despair and moments of elation, in the end, the lesson was learned, and the heart remained true.

I couldn't help but chuckle at the series of events that unfolded. Little did I know, it was just the beginning of a lifetime of unexpected twists and turns.

CHAPTER 3

WHO NEVER TAKES HIS WIFE ON A SCHEDULED HONEYMOON

Woe is a word that has been around a long time. It appears at least 100 times in the Bible. Some of the many definitions of the word are: misery, suffering, trouble, pain, disaster, depression, distress, grief, agony, gloom, sadness, hardship, sorrow, anguish, misfortune, unhappiness, heartache, heartbreak, adversity, dejection, wretchedness.

However, there can be additional circumstances that a husband or boyfriend can experience that go along with the above such as: "the look" which is a hard glare that conveys much of the above and also the silent treatment which can last many days. Then there are actions like being maneuvered into a position where most of the above is unavoidable. It can also be something that is self-inflicted as the following episode will note.

This chapter's heading narrates a chronicle of agony endured by a man who failed to take his beloved wife on an exquisite honeymoon, one that was meticulously organized beforehand, proximate to their wedding day, and officially christened as their honeymoon.

As I approached the end of my college education, my beloved and I tied the knot on a beautiful Saturday evening. Alas, my studies beckoned, and I had to return to class on Monday. Therefore, we both agreed that a honeymoon would have to wait for a more opportune time.

We tied the knot on a beautiful Saturday evening, just six weeks shy of my graduation from college. With my Monday morning classes looming over us, a traditional honeymoon seemed like a distant dream. Instead, we opted to spend our first night of wedded bliss at the only motel in a town roughly 40 miles from campus.

The next day, we decided to take a leisurely drive back to our little apartment and enjoy the scenic route through a state park named Montauk. As we strolled around, admiring the fish hatchery and observing the anglers trying their luck, we basked in the newlywed glow. It was a lovely afternoon, but all too soon it was time to hit the road again and return to our humble abode.

As the years passed by, we embarked on several trips that could have been considered honeymoons, just the two of us, exploring new places and creating cherished memories. However, none of them were planned in advance as a proper honeymoon. I recall a delightful trip to the Oktoberfest in Munich when I was serving in the Army stationed in Germany, but my wife never considered it a true honeymoon.

Despite these trips, the fact that we never had a proper honeymoon continued to weigh on my wife's mind, and she would often remind me of it in front of our friends. She would scoff at the idea that a fish hatchery was a romantic honeymoon destination and longed for the kind of honeymoon that she had always dreamed of much to the agreement of the other wives. The other husbands generally would make some comment like "wow, why didn't I think of that?" All I could do was to try to explain the situation and then come up with the brilliant (or so I thought) statement that our whole marriage had been one long honeymoon

It seems like your attempts at humor didn't quite land with your wife, despite your best efforts. It's understandable that she may have felt disappointed about not having a traditional honeymoon, but it's important to find a way to address her feelings in a respectful and compassionate manner. Perhaps, in the future, you could plan a special trip or experience that she would consider a "real" honeymoon, and make it clear that it is a special occasion for the two of you.

This is a case of perpetual woe due to the circumstances and could have been prevented in hindsight if I had simply said before any of the trips that was to be our honeymoon. There are degrees of woe but the lesson here is **have a real honeymoon!**

CHAPTER 4

DOESN'T THINK THROUGH THE FIRST FEW DAYS OF MARRIAGE.

Woe is a word that has been around for a long time. It appears over 100 times in the Bible. Some of the many definitions of the word are: misery, suffering, trouble, pain, disaster, depression, distress, grief, agony, gloom, sadness, hardship, sorrow, anguish, misfortune, unhappiness, heartache, heartbreak, adversity, dejection, wretchedness.

However, there can be additional circumstances that a husband or boyfriend can experience with their significant other that go along with the above. Open communication can resolve some of these conflicts—others take a more subtle yet intense form.

One such example is what I call "the look," which is a piercing, hard glare that conveys much of the above, and the man now understands that something is amiss and more woe will follow. Another tactic employed by some women is the silent treatment which can last for days on end. It is a powerful tool that can create loneliness and leave the man wondering what he did wrong and when it will ever end.

Then there are insidious tactics—like maneuvers that seem innocent enough but put a man in a vulnerable position. Some could be called external, involving the transferring or sharing of woe. It should be noted that most of the woe incurred by a man is what would be called self-inflicted, where even a small misstep can lead to monumental amounts of woe. This episode will address a self-inflicted woe.

Today's lesson is for those newly married men who need to give thought to their actions in the first few days of marriage. There are three parts to this.

The first part is laundry. Now this is not an exactly romantic discussion but here were the facts. Prior to our marriage while I was still attending college I came home right before the wedding with a duffle bag of dirty laundry thinking my mom would do it like many other visits from college. I should have known that with all the pre-marriage activities that it just wasn't going to be possible for her to get to it. So, this duffle bag of dirty laundry traveled back with my new wife and I to our tiny apartment to start our wonderful married life.

My dear wife was not aware of this start to married life until I unloaded our car. I got the first of some words of woe like "what were you thinking of—that your poor mother would do all that? and now I have to do it?" I really didn't have any good excuse but did round up some quarters for her to use at the laundry mat. For the rest of our married life she would regale her friends about this incident that started her marriage. I think she did this to get the expected responses such as "What a way to start a marriage! I hope you told him what you thought! and You should have made him do it!" This always seemed to get a chuckle from her friends. I never saw it as amusing as they did.

The second part of this has to do with thank you notes. My wife was very diligent regarding thank you notes for the wedding gifts that we had received. She might have even started them while she was doing laundry. It seemed like we got a lot of Corning cook ware. I remember taking several pieces back to the local hardware store that sold most of them to exchange for other items. After my wife had completed several of the notes, she gave me a bunch to mail as I was heading off to class.

The woe started about three or four weeks later when my wife was headed to the cleaners with my coat among other items and went through the pockets only to find that I had forgotten to mail the thank you notes. On getting back to our apartment I was hit with a lot of woe for this major error. I could not come up with any good reason why I had done such a horrible deed and suffered the tongue lashing which in hind sight was well deserved. This was another subject that was passed around later to her friends right along with the laundry problem with the same comments. I just put my head down and tried to not get close to those conversations.

The third item has to do with my compassion and kindness. One would expect that with this start of an explanation that there would be no woe involved. However, there was. On the second day of our marriage I had to be in a 7:30 am class. Yes, this was one of those that was only offered at that time and I needed it for graduation. I would have leave well before 7:00 to get over to my fraternity house which was located right across the street from the campus, get parked and then hike across campus to my class. If I was lucky to be a little ahead of time, I would dash in to the dining area and grab a pastry and maybe some coffee.

Because I was leaving so early and not wanting to bother my new wife I told her the night before that she did not to get up to fix me breakfast. Yes, folks this was back in the day when wives were expected and looked forward to fixing meals for the man or the house. Little did I know that my wife took this to mean all the time or whenever she felt like it! I will say she did fix breakfast quite often but as the years went by it became obvious that my words about not fixing breakfast came back to haunt me.

I think she was on the forefront of women's liberation somewhat but we didn't know it at the time. Because I was normally in a hurry to get off to class or later to work I would often get a quick bowl of cereal and maybe some toast and get out the door. I will say that we did come to a reasonable agreement for her in that I would get breakfast prepared by when she felt like it. So, this ended up being a lifelong woe that had to be endured.

Men, take heart with these lessons and be prepared for them. Of course, the first two were by a blunder-headed person who was not thinking and were definitely self-inflicted. The last one ended up being that way even though it started with great kindness.

CHAPTER 5

WHO IS NOT PREPARED FOR THE SHARING OF WOE

Woe is a word that has been around for a long time. It appears at least 100 times in the Bible. Some of the many definitions of the word are: misery, suffering, trouble, pain, disaster, depression, distress, grief, agony, gloom, sadness, hardship, sorrow, anguish, misfortune, unhappiness, heartache, heartbreak, adversity, dejection, wretchedness.

However, there can be additional circumstances that a husband or boyfriend can experience with their significant other that go along with the above. Open communication can resolve some of these conflicts—others take a more subtle yet intense form.

One such example is what I call "the look," which is a piercing, stern glare that conveys much of the above, and the man now understands that something is amiss and more woe will follow. Another tactic employed by some women is the silent treatment which can last for days on end. It is a powerful tool that can create loneliness and leave the man wondering what he did wrong and when it will ever end.

Then there are insidious tactics—like maneuvers that seem innocent enough but put a man in a vulnerable position. Some could be called external, involving the transferring or sharing of woe. It should be noted that most of the woe incurred by a man is what would be called self-inflicted, where even a small misstep can lead to monumental amounts of woe. This episode will address a shared woe.

This will be discussion on the Transfer and Sharing of Woe. Every man must realize that when woe occurs in another's (his wife's) life, it will most probably be transferred or at least certainly shared with the man. This takes shape in many ways—car problems, computer problems, child issues, etc. Sometimes this transfer of woe isn't necessarily a supreme occurrence, as will be noted in the following paragraphs.

As I delved deeper into the mysteries of male-female dynamics, one principle stood out above all others: The Transfer of Woe. Simply put, when one member of a couple experiences hardship or distress, it's almost inevitable that the other will soon find themselves in the same boat.

Take, for instance, the issue of car trouble. It might seem like a minor inconvenience at first—a flat tire, a dead battery, or an odd clunking noise. But before long, that woe has been transferred to the husband, who suddenly finds himself tinkering under the hood or frantically searching for a replacement part.

Or consider the realm of technology. When a computer or smartphone starts acting up, it's not just a source of frustration for the wife - it's a harbinger of doom for the husband, who knows that he'll soon be called upon to provide technical support, no matter how arcane the problem.

Many years ago, in the first couple of months of our marriage, my dear wife announced at breakfast that she was going to make an apple pie for dinner. My mouth started watering immediately, and this sounded like a wonderful idea.

I was only working a short distance from our house at the time on a big construction site and was able to get home shortly after five. As I walked into the house toward the kitchen, where I knew my new bride would be diligently at work, I announced that I was home. As I entered the kitchen, something whizzed past my ear, hit the wall, and dropped into the wastebasket.

When I looked down, I saw about three wads of dough, and with this, I heard all sorts of woe being described by my wife, who was very mad and almost in tears. She had been trying to prepare pie dough and get it rolled out for a pie crust and was failing miserably. Now pie crust seemed to be a natural thing for her mother, and my mother and my wife had helped them in the past and was sure it was not a hard task. Her woe was now **transferred and shared with** me.

As a husband, I always strived to be kind and supportive of my dear wife. And so, when she expressed a desire for a homemade pie with a flaky, buttery crust, I was more than happy to oblige.

But oh, what a task it proved to be! Together, we toiled in the kitchen, measuring and mixing, rolling and crimping, until at last, we had two crusts that were, to put it kindly, less than perfect. They were lumpy, thick, and decidedly unattractive, but I told her they were fine. After all, it was the effort that counted, right?

As time went on, my wife's skills in the kitchen improved, and her crusts became more and more acceptable. But even then, there were times when they were less than perfect, and our marriage was tested once again.

And yet, we persevered. We laughed at our failures, celebrated our successes, and always remembered that the most important ingredient in any dish was love. Eventually, we discovered the joys of store-bought crusts, and our lives were forever changed.

But even in these dark moments, there is a glimmer of hope. For as the woe is passed back and forth between partners, there is also a sense of shared burden, a recognition that no one person has to bear the weight of the world alone. And in that sense, the Transfer and Sharing of Woe can be a source of strength and resilience rather than just another frustration to be endured.

This is the type of woe transfer/share that has to be accepted without grief and worked through—of course, not all can be accepted as graciously as this one.

CHAPTER 6

WHO DOES NOT TAKE IT EASY AT THE CHRISTMAS PARTY

Woe is a word that has been around for a long time. It appears over 100 times in the Bible. Some of the many definitions of the word are: "misery, suffering, trouble, pain, disaster, depression, distress, grief, agony, gloom, sadness, hardship, sorrow, anguish, misfortune, unhappiness, heartache, heartbreak, adversity, dejection, wretchedness".

However, there can be additional circumstances that a husband or boyfriend can experience with their significant other that go along with the above. Open communication can resolve some of these conflicts—others take a subtler yet intense form.

One such example is what I call "the look," which is a piercing, hard glare that conveys much of the above, and the man now understands that something is amiss and more we will follow. Another tactic employed by some women is the silent treatment which can last for days on end. It is a powerful tool that can create loneliness and leave the man wondering what he did wrong and when it will ever end.

Then there are insidious tactics— like maneuvers that seem innocent enough but put a man in a vulnerable position. Some could be called external, involving the transferring or sharing of woe. It should be noted that most of the woe incurred by a man is what would be called self-inflicted, where even a small misstep can lead to monumental amounts of woe. This episode will address a self-inflicted woe.

The air was thick with excitement and anticipation as the days leading up to the annual Christmas party at the company I worked for drew nearer. We were living near the bustling city of Sacramento. The weather that day was nice and warm, as it should have been in California. The skies were painted in a vibrant shade of blue, with the sun shining brightly and casting a warm, welcoming glow on everything in sight. It was the perfect day for a celebration, and everyone could feel the excitement buzzing in the air. And this particular event was the one that every staff member eagerly looked forward to. It was the perfect opportunity to indulge in some scrumptious, catered food and dance the night away to the soulful tunes of a live band. The festive cheer was palpable, and the buzz of excitement was electrifying. The stage was set for a night that would be etched into our memories for years to come.

As a young and ambitious professional, my salary was not yet at the level of the seasoned employees. However, that did not prevent me from enjoying the company's lavish Christmas party, where champagne flowed freely, and glasses were constantly raised in cheerful toasts. While the champagne was provided at no cost, the bar also offered a tempting selection of other drinks for a nominal fee.

In the days leading up to the much-awaited Christmas party, my wife transformed our humble abode into a winter wonderland with decorations that were nothing short of magical. The centerpiece of it all was the freshly cut Christmas tree, which I had propped up in a sturdy bucket filled with rocks—a frugal solution I had always used. Despite its slight wobbliness, it looked solid enough to hold up the heavy ornaments that my wife meticulously arranged with an eagle eye for detail. The babysitter who arrived that evening couldn't help but compliment us on the breathtaking sight that greeted her.

The festivities of the evening continued to soar, with the jovial atmosphere only getting better as time passed. We sat at a table of eight, where we indulged in delectable dishes and an abundance of toasts. Dancing was in full swing, and the champagne flowed freely. Despite the champagne not being the best quality, my buddies and I kept guzzling it down, knowing that it was easier on the wallet than any other beverage. But our fun was cut short by our wives, who started to remind us to slow down and take it easy. If only we had heeded their advice.

The joyous night came to an end as the band played their last tune, and the party-goers started to make their way back home. My wife, being the responsible one, took the wheel and drove us home as I was feeling the effects of the unlimited champagne. We dropped off our friends and headed back to our humble abode. However, as we entered our home, something caught our attention. We quickly realized that our beautifully decorated Christmas tree had fallen over, leaving behind a trail of broken ornaments and shattered memories. It was a sight to behold and an unfortunate end to an otherwise memorable night.

The air in the house was immediately thick with tension, and my heart sank as soon as I noticed the fallen tree. The once-beautiful decorations were now scattered on the floor, a shattered mess. The babysitter was profusely apologizing noting that it had just fallen over by itself, but it was clear that this was not going to alleviate the anger brewing within my wife.

In a daze, I accompanied the babysitter back to her house and tried to collect myself on the walk back. But as soon as I stepped inside, I was met with a barrage of harsh words and criticism. My wife was not holding back, and I was in no position to defend myself. Thankfully, the alcohol and exhaustion overtook me, and I was allowed to hit the bed and had no problem drifting off into a deep sleep, leaving the mess for tomorrow's headache.

The next morning, I was reminded of the age-old adage: "What goes up must come down." The cheap champagne I had so gleefully imbibed was wreaking havoc on my system, causing me to feel like I had been hit by a freight train. The bathroom became my new best friend as I stumbled back and forth, attempting to quell the churning in my stomach. My dear wife was ever-present, offering her "words of wisdom," which, at that moment, sounded like nails on a chalkboard. The throbbing in my head felt like a marching band was practicing inside my skull, and the only relief I could find was in the consumption of several aspirins.

My hangover was relentless and unforgiving, and it seemed like every step I took was a test of my endurance. As I stumbled through the house, my wife's voice followed me like a persistent shadow, reminding me of my folly from the night before. The fallen Christmas tree was still lying on the floor, and I knew that I needed to address it. But every movement was an effort, and it was well past noon before I was able to summon the strength to begin cleaning up the shattered ornaments and twisted branches.

I was able to summon a friend to help me get the tree upright once more, and we were able to craft a fine wooden frame to hold it firmly in place. Braces were added against the trunk, and sturdy legs were laid flat on the floor to ensure that the tree would remain upright for the rest of the holiday season. I couldn't help but feel proud of our work, but my friend was the one who received the most praise for his carpentry skills. The presence of my friend gave my wife some confidence that things were improving. I had to endure him humming the tune to "Oh Christmas Tree, Oh Christmas Tree" then and in the days afterword.

It was a relief to finally put an end to the woe that had been haunting me since the tree had fallen over. My wife, who had been particularly vocal in her criticisms of my tree-erecting abilities, was finally able to relax and enjoy the holiday season once more. The tree stood tall and proud, a beacon of Christmas cheer in our home.

After that memorable Christmas party, champagne held a different place in my heart. The thought of it made my stomach churn, my head throb with pain, and my memories flood back to that disastrous night. The spilled tree and broken ornaments were one thing, but the hangover was an entirely different beast. It was a harsh lesson learned, but one that stuck with me for years to come. I became a moderate drinker, sipping cautiously at the bubbly liquid during toasts and only indulging in moderation. My wife had been a guiding force in this new era of responsible drinking, her wise words ringing in my ears long after that fateful night.

Despite the unfortunate incident, we managed to salvage a memorable Christmas. As time passed and we reminisced with friends, the story evolved, with the fallen tree becoming the centerpiece rather than my overindulgence in champagne.

This is a clear case of self-inflicted woe and perhaps more consequences than normal. Remember, put the tree up well, and do not drink a lot of cheap champagne! This is about a good example of self-inflicted woe as there is!

CHAPTER 7

WHO THINKS HE CAN GO JOGGING

Woe is a word that has been around for a long time. It appears at least 100 times in the Bible. Some of the many definitions of the word are: misery, suffering, trouble, pain, disaster, depression, distress, grief, agony, gloom, sadness, hardship, sorrow, anguish, misfortune, unhappiness, heartache, heartbreak, adversity, dejection, wretchedness.

However, there can be additional circumstances that a husband or boyfriend can experience with their significant other that go along with the above. Open communication can resolve some of these conflicts—others take a more subtle yet intense form.

One such example is what I call "the look," which is a piercing, hard glare that conveys much of the above, and the man now understands that something is amiss and more woe will follow. Another tactic employed by some women is the silent treatment which can last for days on end. It is a powerful tool that can create loneliness and leave the man wondering what he did wrong and when it will ever end.

Then there are insidious tactics— like maneuvers that seem innocent enough but put a man in a vulnerable position. Some could be called external, involving the transferring or sharing of woe. It should be noted that most of the woe incurred by a man is what would be called self-inflicted, where even a small misstep can lead to monumental amounts of woe. This episode will address a self-inflicted woe.

Many years ago, while living in sunny Southern California and enjoying the nice weather, I gazed out, watching the joggers breeze by with seemingly boundless energy, and I couldn't help but feel a twinge of envy. After all, who wouldn't want to feel fit, healthy, and full of vitality?

But as I considered taking up jogging myself, I faced a formidable obstacle—when to fit it into my busy schedule. With work, family commitments, and other obligations, finding time for a new activity seemed almost impossible.

And yet, something within me urged me to give it a try. I knew that jogging could have a transformative effect on my life, helping me shed a few extra pounds and boosting my overall well-being. But how to make it work?

The answer, it seemed, was to rise earlier and hit the pavement before the demands of the day set in. It was a daunting prospect, but one that I knew I had to tackle head-on.

My wife, though supportive in her own way, had her reservations. She cautioned me to take it slow and not to disrupt her own precious sleep schedule with my early morning ventures. But I was undeterred - the lure of a healthier, happier life was too strong to ignore. And so, with determination in my heart and running shoes on my feet, I set out to make jogging a part of my daily routine.

So, I got up at the crack of dawn—around 5:00 am or so and threw on some running attire—OK, it was a ratty T-shirt and old shorts because surely no one would see me. I sneaked out the front door closing it quietly, did a few stretches, and started off on a slow jog. I forgot to mention that I was still about half-asleep but thought I was somewhat alert.

I headed out into the street and was going to hang a right at the first intersection, which was only about 50 yards from the house. As I was going around that corner, my left foot stepped on a slight difference in the pavement and gutter, and I fell immediately to that harsh pavement. With this brilliant maneuver, I sprained my left ankle and skinned up both knees, and both hands, including the back of one. There was instant woe in the form of pain, anguish, distress, dejection, and several others.

I looked around to see if anyone saw me offer assistance, but I was forced to get back up on my own. Even though my ankle hurt and I was only bleeding a little, I gave a couple of steps and figured I was surely strong enough to carry on at least another few blocks. This macho man was not going to let a little mishap slow him down. I was limping pretty badly but got another block, and then I incurred a severe cramp in my right calf because I favored the left ankle so much. Now I had a real problem because both legs were causing woe. It is nearly impossible to jog or walk when you have to favor both legs. I was able to get turned around and really hobbled slowly back to my front door. I was advising myself and anyone else all the way about how wretched this was.

Now it was still early because I had not been gone from the house for only about 15 minutes and unfortunately, I was not really quiet when I went back in the house because I was making a lot of noise with my hobbling, but I did speak a little softer in expressing my pain. However, as I got back into the bedroom and started trying to get clothes and running shoes off, I made a lot of noise and woke up my wife.

There are those in this world who wake with ease, their eyes opening to the dawn with a sense of wonder and joy. Alas, my dear wife is not one of them. Even in the best of circumstances, waking her from her slumber is an endeavor fraught with peril, for it sets in motion a series of events that can be most vexing indeed.

As I floundered about in pain, my wife was roused from her peaceful repose with a start. Her first reaction was one of annoyance, for how dare I disrupt her precious sleep? And yet, as she beheld my sorry state, she realized that something was truly amiss.

Her concern was palpable, but so too was her frustration. How could I have been so foolish as to hurt myself? And why hadn't I returned home immediately after my fall? Such questions were hurled at me with a ferocity that belied her love and cared for my well-being.

And so, as I lay there, wracked with pain and beset by my wife's chiding, I couldn't help but wonder if it was worth it. Was it worth the trouble, the worry, the woe of waking her from her slumber? Only time would tell, but for now, all I could do was endure and hoped that my injuries would heal swiftly.

In the aftermath of my crisis, I found myself in need of aid. Blood flowed from my wounds, and I knew that I could not staunch the bleeding on my own. And so, with trepidation, I turned to the one person who could help me in my time of need.

She did not offer words of endearment, nor did she shower me with praise for waking her from her slumber. Instead, she tended to my wounds with a cool detachment, as though it were a mere inconvenience to be dealt with. When I finally got cleaned up and showered on one foot for the most part, I was able to get a bit to eat and then drive to work.

As the morning wore on, I found myself navigating the trials of daily life with a sense of unease. My colleagues at work asked me what had happened, and I could see the mirth in their eyes as they listened to my tale. To be the butt of their jokes, to give them a reason to laugh at my expense, was yet another burden to bear.

While the idea of jogging was a good one, the good Lord must have known it wasn't for me. Years have passed since that fateful day, and I have not once considered taking up jogging again, save for dire circumstances such as fleeing danger or avoiding a downpour. For it is clear that some things are not meant for all, and in my case, jogging is one such thing.

CHAPTER 8

WHO EVER ASKS HIS WIFE TO HUSTLE

Woe is a word that has been around a long time. It appears over 100 times in the Bible. Some of the many definitions of the word are misery, suffering, trouble, pain, disaster, depression, distress, grief, agony, gloom, sadness, hardship, sorrow, anguish, misfortune, unhappiness, heartache, heartbreak, adversity, dejection, wretchedness.

However, there can be additional circumstances that a husband can experience that go along with the above such as: "the look," which is a hard glare that conveys much of the above, and the silent treatment which can last many days. Then there are actions like being maneuvered into a position where most of the above is unavoidable.

Then there are insidious tactics— like maneuvers that seem innocent enough but put a man in a vulnerable position. Some could be called external, involving the transferring or sharing of woe. It should be noted that most of the woe incurred by a man is what would be called self-inflicted, where even a small misstep can lead to monumental amounts of woe. This episode will address a self-inflicted woe.

Hustle is a common word often found in athletic events where a coach wants a player to get with it or really move fast and energetically. In the military it is used frequently by drill sergeants. It is not a word that works well with a wife. The woe experienced today is by a man who was seated comfortably at his breakfast table with milk on his Cheerios when he realized that he had not gotten the morning newspaper.

As he looks up, he spots his wife standing in the doorway to the breakfast area. He forgets that his wife is really not a morning person, but one that needs two cups of coffee and at least 30 minutes of quiet solitude in order to face the day. This is unlike her mother who loved to sing and make noise in the kitchen before sunrise. But this man, in his dire need for the paper, innocently and kindly asks her to "hustle" and fetch the paper, all while his cereal grows soggier by the second. Little did he know that this one word would unleash a storm of woe upon him.

Alas, his plea for assistance delivered in the most innocent of tones - only served to unleash a torrent of woe. The once-peaceful atmosphere was shattered by a barrage of hot, angry words that scorched the air and set the husband's heart aflutter. The wife made sure to drive home the gravity of the situation with repeated verbal lashings, leaving the husband with no doubt that he had erred greatly. Her words rang in his ears like a siren's call "I am not going out in my nightgown" and "get it yourself". The poor husband was left to face the consequences of his ill-timed request.

As he scurried away to the front walk with his head lowered, returning with a clutched damp newspaper as if it were a precious gem, he couldn't help but pray for a speedy end to the brewing storm of disapproval. Perhaps if he humbly presented her with the coveted front section, her wrath would soften before he even dared to tackle his soggy Cheerios. But for now, he simply trudged forward, feeling like a wounded soldier on a treacherous battlefield of domestic conflict.

Regrettably, his offering of the front section did little to assuage the brewing tempest that was his spouse's displeasure. As he tentatively took a spoonful of his now-soggy Cheerios, he knew that silence was the only permissible response in such situations. Attempting to reason or provide any form of logical explanation would only add fuel to the already raging fire. That lesson had been learned the hard way, through countless past experiences of similar "woe". It was a painful realization that left him feeling as though he were navigating a minefield with no discernible path to safety.

Perhaps, with the right approach and a generous helping of humor,-this subject of woe could eventually have been addressed. But this would be a precarious path to tread, fraught with potential missteps and landmines. The safer route is to avoid any situation that could lead to woe altogether. And above all, one must never, under any circumstances, request that their wife hustle. For that, dear friend, is a surefire recipe for woe that is best avoided at all costs.

CHAPTER 9

WHO IS NOT AWARE OF HIS WIFE'S REAL SHOPPING PLAN

Woe is a word that has been around for a long time. It appears at least 100 times in the Bible. Some of the many definitions of the word are: misery, suffering, trouble, pain, disaster, depression, distress, grief, agony, gloom, sadness, hardship, sorrow, anguish, misfortune, unhappiness, heartache, heartbreak, adversity, dejection, wretchedness.

However, there can be additional circumstances that a husband or boyfriend can experience with their significant other that go along with the above. Open communication can resolve some of these conflicts—others take a subtler yet intense form.

One such example is what I call "the look," which is a piercing, hard glare that conveys much of the above, and the man now understands that something is amiss and more we will follow. Another tactic employed by some women is the silent treatment which can last for days on end. It is a powerful tool that can create loneliness and leave the man wondering what he did wrong and when it will ever end.

Then there are insidious tactics— like maneuvers that seem innocent enough but put a man in a vulnerable position. Some could be called external, involving the transferring or sharing of woe. It should be noted that most of the woe incurred by a man is what would be called self-inflicted, where even a small misstep can lead to monumental amounts of woe. This episode will address an inflicted woe.

On a recent drive with my wife, she remarked that we needed to make a stop at a department store for her to purchase a couple of bras. Naively assuming that this would be a simple and swift affair, I volunteered to remain in the car and catch up on a ballgame, as I believed this to be a vastly preferable option to entering the treacherous terrain of the lingerie department. However, my wife had other ideas, insisting that I accompany her and browse the men's section for a few minutes while she completed her shopping. Looking back, this should have served as the first warning sign that trouble was on the horizon.

Before delving into my tale, it is important to note that most men, myself included, harbor an aversion towards shopping for clothes, a sentiment that starkly contrasts with the disposition of women. In the event that I find myself in dire need of an article of clothing, such as when I am down to my last pair of serviceable underwear, I will quickly dash into a store, locate my size, make my purchase, and exit posthaste. Women, on the other hand, possess a proclivity for spending hours browsing for ostensibly the same item and often expect their husbands to adopt a similar outlook.

As I hastened away from the lingerie section, eager to put as much distance as possible between myself and the sensuous undergarments, I meandered over to the men's department. To pacify my spouse and perhaps make her feel like I was putting in the effort, I ambled around for a bit, perusing various articles of clothing. However, after a while, I began to grow uneasy. My wife had yet to return, and I could not seem to locate her. My anxiety mounting, I retraced my steps to the lingerie section, but to my dismay, she was nowhere in sight. In a last-ditch effort, I retreated once again to the men's department, praying that she had simply strayed into another area of the store.

Out of nowhere, my wife appeared by my side and dragged me to the shirts and trousers section, shoving all kinds of garments into my hands with certainty that they would meet my taste. I could sense that I was being led into a trap, but my protests fell on deaf ears. I weighed my options and decided to take the path of least resistance, ending up purchasing three shirts and two pairs of trousers, all while managing to keep a pleasant expression on my face and avoid any grumbling or griping.

This incident is a perfect illustration of how a man can be unwittingly maneuvered into a troublesome situation of woe. It is important to always be vigilant when accompanying your spouse on shopping trips, as you never know when they might try to drag you into a clothing store against your will to shop for your clothes,

CHAPTER 10

WHO IS NOT PREPARED FOR THE TRANSFER OF WOE

Woe is a word that has been around for a long time. It appears over 100 times in the Bible. Some of the many definitions of the word are misery, suffering, trouble, pain, disaster, depression, distress, grief, agony, gloom, sadness, hardship, sorrow, anguish, misfortune, unhappiness, heartache, heartbreak, adversity, dejection, wretchedness.

However, there can be additional circumstances that a husband can experience that go along with the above such as: "the look" which is a hard glare that conveys much of the above and also can result in the silent treatment which can last for a long time. Then there are actions like being maneuvered into a position where most of the above is unavoidable.

This will be a discussion on the Transfer or Sharing of Woe. Every man must realize that when woe occurs in another's (his wife's) life, it will most probably be transferred or at least certainly shared with the man. This takes the shape in many ways—car problems, computer problems, child issues, etc. Sometimes this transfer of woe isn't necessarily a supreme occurrence as will be noted in the following paragraphs.

Back when we resided in a modern neighborhood situated in the southern region of Denver, we actively participated in various community activities. Among the groups we joined was one spearheaded by a group of enterprising wives who organized a monthly Gourmet Club rendezvous, where we would gather at someone's home for a themed dinner party. Our taste buds were tantalized with various cuisines such as Italian, Chinese, German, Seafood, and more. Each couple was given a specific dish to prepare, ranging from appetizers to soups, vegetables, and everything in between. During the German-themed soirée, we were tasked with creating a scrumptious dessert that would leave everyone craving for more.

Our initial task was to choose what delightful dessert to prepare. We scoured through multiple cookbooks in search of the perfect treat, until we stumbled upon a classic German Chocolate Cake, which held a special place in my heart from my days of serving in the Army in Germany. The Colorado Cache Cookbook provided an excellent recipe that we couldn't resist trying.

The following is what we prepared for the recipe to take with us to share:
Gourmet Club, German, October 1 1983

BLACK FOREST CAKE

1. Find a reasonable recipe. Veronica's Kirshe Torte on page 337 of "Colorado Cache Cookbook" looks good.
2. Dispatch husband to find Kirshwassar (Cherry Brandy). Who keeps that around?
3. Bake cake as per recipe. Watch cake fall to resemble a flat brownie. Drink Kirshwassar.
4. Call husband (**this is the transfer of woe**). Have him go to 1500 East Colfax to Vollmar's Bakery and get a Black Forest Cake. Warn him not to stop at Zack's next door for drinks.
5. Put cake on another container so no one knows it's from a bakery. Brag a bit about how hard it was to make.
6. Give everyone this easy-to-follow recipe.

Combined efforts of Howard and Linda Henry

The emotional burden in this situation was apparent as my wife called me with distressing news. Though worried, we managed to pull through and make the dessert work. No one at the gathering had any inkling of the hiccup, and we even received several compliments on how delicious the cake tasted. Everyone raved about the recipe, oblivious to the hurdles we had to overcome to make it happen.

Indeed, in this particular scenario, the transferor sharing of woe was not a significant issue that would have a lasting impact. It was crucial to address and overcome the distress experienced by my wife at that moment, but once the problem was resolved, we were able to move past it and enjoy the evening with our friends. While the situation may have caused some temporary stress and concern, it did not leave a lingering impact on our lives or relationships.

CHAPTER 11

WHO TRIES TO USE LOGIC WITH HIS WIFE

Woe is a word that has been around for a long time. It appears at least 100 times in the Bible. Some of the many definitions of the word are misery, suffering, trouble, pain, disaster, depression, distress, grief, agony, gloom, sadness, hardship, sorrow, anguish, misfortune, unhappiness, heartache, heartbreak, adversity, dejection, wretchedness.

However, there can be additional circumstances that a husband can experience that goes along with the above such as: "the look," which is a hard glare that conveys much of the above, and also the silent treatment, which can last many days. Then there are actions like trying to apply Logic with your wife that results in all of the above.

In this episode, we will discuss the troubles that a man faces when he tries to apply Logic while explaining a seemingly simple task to his wife.

Recently, we faced a significant setback when our 20-year-old Maytag washer stopped working with a loud "clump" sound. We found out that repairing it would cost almost as much as buying a new one. So, we began our hunt for a new washer and dryer, and after visiting various stores, we decided to buy a Kenmore from Sears. The machine had simple controls, which we preferred since we didn't want to deal with complicated settings that we would never understand.

Fast forward a couple of weeks, and my wife requested that I load and start the washer. Thinking it was a simple task, I began to add the detergent when she appeared and immediately halted my efforts. Apparently, I was doing it wrong, and her way—letting the machine fill up with water and running it for a few minutes before adding the detergent—was the only way. When I mentioned that the instructions didn't mention such a technique, it only added to the woes, as she was insistent that her mother had taught her this method, and that's just how it was going to be done. It's a tricky situation when a husband tries to logically explain a task to his wife, especially when her mother's teachings are involved. Despite showing her the manual, which contradicted her method, I still found it easier to just do it her way to avoid any further woe. In fact, when I tried to humorously acknowledge my new-found understanding of her method in the future, it only earned me a "now you're learning" look. So, husbands, be warned—sometimes it's best to just go with the flow and keep the peace.

I did regain a little dignity in this matter at times. When she was not around and I had to wash some clothes, I would follow the instruction manual and amazingly the clothes came out clean, at least to me

It's important for men to understand that Logic doesn't always prevail in discussions with their wives. The moment the infamous phrase, "That's how my mother taught me," is uttered, it's time to back down and concede. Using phrases such as "that's just common sense" is also a big no-no, as it will only lead to further frustration and woe, even if you are in the right. It's best to approach the situation with patience and understanding and to always be willing to compromise. Remember, a happy wife is a happy life.

It's important to communicate with your partner and share your thoughts and opinions; it's also important to be respectful and understanding of their views and preferences. Relationships require compromise and understanding from both parties. Instead of assuming that your way is the only logical way, try to understand your partner's perspective and work together to find a solution that works for both of you. Remember that logic is sometimes a fragile approach

CHAPTER 12

WHO THINKS HE IS LOST

Woe is a word that has been around for a long time. It appears over 100 times in the Bible. Some of the many definitions of the word are: misery, suffering, trouble, pain, disaster, depression, distress, grief, agony, gloom, sadness, hardship, sorrow, anguish, misfortune, unhappiness, heartache, heartbreak, adversity, dejection, wretchedness.

However, there can be additional circumstances that a husband or boyfriend can experience with their significant other that go along with the above. Open communication can resolve some of these conflicts—others take a more subtle yet intense form.

One such example is what I call "the look," which is a piercing, hard glare that conveys much of the above, and the man now understands that something is amiss and more woe will follow. Another tactic employed by some women is the silent treatment which can last for days on end. It is a powerful tool that can create loneliness and leave the man wondering what he did wrong and when it will ever end.

Then there are insidious tactics— like maneuvers that seem innocent enough but put a man in a vulnerable position. Some could be called external, involving the transferring or sharing of woe. It should be noted that most of the woe incurred by a man is what would be called self-inflicted, where even a small misstep can lead to monumental amounts of woe. This episode will address a self-inflicted woe.

There are times when a man is driving along when he realizes that he is not sure where he is or if he missed a road or sign or anything that gives him that uneasy feeling that he might be slightly or really lost. Sometimes, he will probably now be on the receiving end of an exchange from his wife, who will say something like—do you know where you are? Or this doesn't look familiar.

This will be addressed in two sections—the first being before GPS and the second after GPS. From this obvious statement, one will know that I am old enough to be on both sides of GPS.

Before GPS, when it became known to all that the man did not know exactly where he was, the wife's first statement would be—why don't you stop and ask someone? Now, this is an affront to any man who would rather drive for miles than be humiliated into going up to someone's house to get directions. I need to note that my wife has no sense of direction-don't tell her to go north or west—that means nothing. Before we were married, she would take the bus to and from work in St. Louis. One day she missed her stop on the way home and was instantly lost when she got off. She hailed a cab, and although he gave her an odd look, he proceeded to drive her around the block to the front of her apartment building.

It is a little easier to endure if there is a convenient gas station, but that almost never happens, or the suggestion is made about 5 miles after passing one. The other problem is if you are in a suburban area or out in the country. Both have issues—the first is getting someone to answer the door in either area. Second, in the country, there are normally one or more a couple of big, mean-looking, and sounding dogs between you and the house. And, of course, there is no one around to hear you yelling for assistance. If it was after dark, compound all the problems by ten. If you are in a "bad" part of town, keep going even if that gets you it a worse part—or pray you to see a policeman.

When you do get to a live person to ask directions, you often get a question—how did you ever get here? Then you have to make them understand where you are going. Then you have to understand their direction, which can give you more woe—like go down that road a little way to the third road on the left, and when it forks, go toward the creek. If you hear anything like that, you do have problems. All of this normally comes with a constant flow of advice from your other half—part of the woe that must be endured.

With the advent of the GPS, a lot of technically savvy drivers will enter the correct info in their GPS before they leave and hope that will be the right information. Most of the time that works. But if the man forgets or does not plan to use the GPS and then gets into a situation where he is not sure of his whereabouts, he will hear the words—do you know where you are? And why don't you use the GPS?

Using GPS isn't always going to fix the issue. One time I was driving our motorhome pulling a car and missed a turn. The GPS lady said to go to the next intersection and do a U-turn! Good luck with that working.

When lost or semi-lost, there will be some amount of woe incurred by the driver for that and more when it is conveyed to the wife. Fortunately, this can be wiped out with great relief when something familiar comes into sight. And even though you might have to drive a long way to get to where you were supposed to go, eventually, some form of happiness will return (if he hasn't been curt with his wife). Men, in order to avoid this type of self-inflected woe, do a little planning before the trip!!

Chapter 13

Who Ever Has to Shop for a Bra for His Wife

Woe is a word that has been around for a long time. It appears at least 100 times in the Bible. Some of the many definitions of the word are: misery, suffering, trouble, pain, disaster, depression, distress, grief, agony, gloom, sadness, hardship, sorrow, anguish, misfortune, unhappiness, heartache, heartbreak, adversity, dejection, wretchedness.

However, there can be additional circumstances that a husband can experience that goes along with the above such as: "the look," which is a hard glare that conveys much of the above, and the silent treatment, which can last many days. Then there are actions like being maneuvered into a position where most of the above are unavoidable.

Today's epistle is on the woes that a man must endure when he has to go shopping for a bra for his wife.

Not long ago, my beloved was admitted to the hospital for an extended period, and she expressed the need for a more accommodating bra. It was evident that the task of acquiring one fell upon me. Now, as a typical husband, I excel in navigating the aisles of a hardware store, but I must admit that delving into the realm of lingerie shopping was uncharted territory for me. As a matter of fact, most husbands tend to steer clear of the lingerie department, fearing that they may be perceived as peculiar or having unsavory proclivities.

My wife had her heart set on a particular brand of bra, and I assumed it would be a straightforward task since Bali bras were widely available in major department stores. However, my confidence was short-lived. As a cautious shopper, I decided to begin my search at Macy's, where I quietly made my way to the lingerie department. To my surprise, the plethora of bras on display left me feeling flustered and confused. I had no idea there were so many different ones in all shapes and colors. And, of course, I couldn't seem to find the Bali brand that my wife had requested.

To compound matters, locating a sales clerk proved to be a challenge, as the department was being attended to by only one clerk, who was busily helping a group of female customers that appeared to know exactly what they were looking for.

After a few moments of feeling lost and uncomfortable, the kind sales clerk must have sensed my unease and offered her assistance. With empathy in her voice, she informed me that Macy's did not carry the Bali bra that my wife desired but that another department store located at the opposite end of the mall did.

Grateful for her guidance, I thanked the clerk and began the long trek to the other end of the mall, determined to find the elusive lingerie department and the Bali bra that my wife had requested. Eventually, after a bit of wandering, I located the department and was relieved to find the Bali brand in stock but could not find my wife's bra in another massive display.

Upon arriving at the lingerie department of the other store, I was relieved to find a couple of sales clerks who appeared to be closer to my age and who didn't judge me for my lack of lingerie knowledge. At this point, I learned that the most effective approach was to appear helpless and hopeless (I'm real good at that) and to seek the guidance of those who knew what they were doing.

Luckily, the helpful clerks were able to locate the Bali bras that I needed, despite their steep price tags, which took me by surprise (far more expensive than a simple screwdriver). Nevertheless, I quickly paid for them, eager to leave the department and make my way back to the hospital where my wife awaited.

My fervent hopes were for an appreciative response from my beloved wife. Her remark about the color was all that was forthcoming. Nevertheless, being a devoted and supportive spouse, I gritted my teeth and kept my frustrations under wraps, praying that I would never have to endure such a daunting task again.

Although the difficulties I encountered during my foray into lingerie shopping were not the most formidable, they were undoubtedly challenging. Nevertheless, this experience taught me the invaluable lesson that sometimes, we must confront unpleasant situations head-on, even if we are loath to do so.

Despite my fervent desire to eschew any future lingerie shopping excursions, I have gleaned valuable insights from my misadventures and shall be well-equipped with the knowledge of where to turn the next time my beloved spouse requires a specific bra. This was a classic case of necessary woe.

Chapter 14

Who Ever Suggests His Wife Needs to get Her Hearing Checked

Woe is a word that has been around for a long time. It appears over 100 times in the Bible. Some of the many definitions of the word are misery, suffering, trouble, pain, disaster, depression, distress, grief, agony, gloom, sadness, hardship, sorrow, anguish, misfortune, unhappiness, heartache, heartbreak, adversity, dejection, wretchedness.

However, there can be additional circumstances that a husband can experience that goes along with the above such as: "the look," which is a hard glare that conveys much of the above, and also the silent treatment, which can last many days. Then there are actions like trying to apply logic with your wife that result in all of the above.

Then there are insidious tactics— like maneuvers that seem innocent enough but put a man in a vulnerable position. Some could be called external, involving the transferring or sharing of woe. It should be noted that most of the woe incurred by a man is what would be called self-inflicted, where even a small misstep can lead to monumental amounts of woe. This episode will address a self-inflicted woe

It is important to understand that hearing loss is a common occurrence as we age, and it is not something to be ashamed of. Denial or avoidance of the issue can lead to further problems down the line. Seeking medical advice from a qualified professional is the best course of action to take.

Ignoring hearing loss can lead to more woe and frustration in the long run. We may find ourselves constantly asking people to repeat themselves or feeling left out of conversations. It's not worth the hassle and discomfort.

So, the next time someone suggests we get our hearing checked, let's take it seriously and consider the potential benefits of hearing aids or other treatments. It may be a small inconvenience now, but it could greatly improve our quality of life in the future.

In today's lesson a man who has been married even a short time will start to hear words like "you need to get your hearing checked". Our response normally has been "it's fine, or it's the TV, or you just need to speak up a little, you are mumbling, or it's the traffic outside", or anything that will take away the possibility that you may be losing your hearing. We try to do this with humor or a smile to convey that we are truly listening. An example of this is to say "huh" and grin. That almost always does not get a smile back. Some of the examples of **woe** normally appear at this point.

I have even gone to the extreme of having my hearing checked. The result was that I had a very mild hearing loss in one ear. I came home with a big flourish waving the results and exclaiming my healthy condition. This was met with extreme skepticism instead of words like "that's great". One can expect to hear strong suggestions get one's hearing checked many times after this

Now it so happens that my wife will often ask me to repeat statements. I have even purposely spoken in a quiet tone of voice to elicit her response. At this point, or in response to her suggestion that I need my hearing checked, I will make the statement that **she needs to get her hearing checked.** At this point, **woe** sets in quickly. There is no hesitation. The glare comes instantly with a very firm "I do not" with louder comments about I am the one that needs it and other unloving statements. I also made the mistake of saying one time that a lot of women wore hearing aids. While this was a very logical and true statement, it had no effect on the situation and brought on more **woe.**

The obvious conclusion to this lesson would be to never ever suggest that you wife needs to have her hearing checked (unless the TV is so loud that your neighbors complain, or your dogs start whining). At the end of all of this there was one obvious conclusion and that I was the only one that needed my hearing checked

While it's important to take care of our hearing and address any potential issues, it's also important to approach the topic sensitively with our loved ones. Instead of suggesting that they have their hearing checked, it may be more effective to express concern for their well-being and suggest that you both get your hearing checked together. This can help reduce any feelings of defensiveness or resistance and show that you are both in it together. Additionally, being proactive about addressing hearing issues can improve communication and quality of life for both partners.

Chapter 15

Who is Not Prepared for His Wife's Weight Gain

Woe is a word that has been around for a long time. It appears over 100 times in the Bible. Some of the many definitions of the word are: misery, suffering, trouble, pain, disaster, depression, distress, grief, agony, gloom, sadness, hardship, sorrow, anguish, misfortune, unhappiness, heartache, heartbreak, adversity, dejection, wretchedness.

However, there can be additional circumstances that a husband or boyfriend can experience with their significant other that go along with the above. Open communication can resolve some of these conflicts—others take a more subtle yet intense form.

One such example is what I call "the look," which is a piercing, hard glare that conveys much of the above, and the man now understands that something is amiss and more we will follow. Another tactic employed by some women is the silent treatment which can last for days on end. It is a powerful tool that can create loneliness and leave the man wondering what he did wrong and when it will ever end.

Then there are insidious tactics— like maneuvers that seem innocent enough but put a man in a vulnerable position. Some could be called external, involving the transferring or sharing of woe. It should be noted that most of the woe incurred by a man is what would be called self-inflicted, where even a small misstep can lead to monumental amounts of woe. This episode will address an inevitable and shared woe.

As the years go by, our bodies inevitably change, and the once youthful figure we once had becomes a distant memory. For many, it can be a difficult and even daunting realization to come to terms with. While men may seem to have an easier time accepting this reality, women, on the other hand, can feel a great deal of pressure to maintain their appearance. Society often perpetuates the idea that a woman's worth is tied to her looks, leaving many feeling inadequate and insecure. However, it's important to remember that beauty comes in all shapes and sizes, and our worth goes far beyond our physical appearance

The way we approach these changes can differ vastly between genders. Men may brush it off with a shrug of the shoulders and a trip to the store to buy some bigger clothes. If we are concerned we may try to diet and exercise first and then go buy the bigger clothes. Women, on the other hand, may become upset, insecure, and feel self-conscious about their appearance.

Men, be warned. This is a sensitive topic, and it's crucial to choose your words carefully. A single misplaced comment could set off a chain reaction of woe and misery that could last for days or even weeks. No matter how well-intentioned your words may be, be cautious, as the outcome may not be what you intended. Even saying "I like you as you are" could mean you like her with her weight gain

As the diet plan comes into play, the husband must tread lightly. The days of indulging in mashed potatoes and gravy, pasta, and juicy steaks will be over. Instead, the table will be filled with salads, vegetables, and lean proteins. The husband will be forced to adjust to this new reality and accept the limited food choices. Complaining about the lack of flavor or portions will only result in a more limited diet. Perhaps, if the husband behaves, he may receive a small reward in the form of a sugar-free cookie. Nonetheless, it is a small price to pay for a healthier lifestyle, and the husband must remember to support and encourage his wife during this process.

As with most things in life, diets are temporary, a fleeting remedy to a much larger issue. A glimmer of hope that quickly fades into the realization that, as humans, we are imperfect creatures prone to indulgence and excess. The weight may come off, but it's only a matter of time before it creeps back on again. And with it comes another round of dieting, another battle against temptation and the alluring scent of freshly baked bread.

As the battle against the bulge continues, the next line of defense is often exercise. Walking is a favorite for many women, as it allows for gentle movement and the fresh air without the discomfort of heavy sweating. And what better way to tackle this challenge than with a fellow sister-in-arms? Finding a friend who is also on the same journey can be a great motivator and offer much-needed support. They can share tips and tricks, offer encouragement when the going gets tough, and make the journey much more enjoyable. Together, they can conquer the road and make strides toward a healthier lifestyle.

Inevitably, if walking fails to produce the desired results, the gym is the next destination for those on the quest for a more svelte figure. The husband is often enlisted in this endeavor, but if his schedule does not permit, finding a suitable workout buddy is a must. If the wife works, this provides the perfect opportunity for the husband to get involved, offering support and encouragement to his beloved partner. The gym approach can work but is often a temporary thing because of schedule, kids, and other activities.

As a loving husband, it is your duty to provide your wife with unwavering support and encouragement throughout her weight loss journey. Patience and understanding will be your greatest allies as the process may take longer than expected. You must learn to be a cheerleader and a motivator and celebrate every small victory achieved along the way.

Inevitably, your wife will have to buy bigger clothes, which can be a sensitive topic. It is important to approach this with compassion and understanding and offer to help with the shopping process. Be prepared for a significant financial investment in new clothes as your wife sheds or likely adds those extra pounds.

As your wife progresses through her journey, it is important to understand that her body may never be the same as it once was. It's essential to help her find acceptance and love for her body at every stage of the journey. With patience, love, and unwavering support, you can help your wife reach a place of body acceptance and self-love.

Inevitable woe is a phenomenon that cannot be avoided in most marriages, and weight gain is one of its prominent manifestations. It is a shared experience that both husband and wife will endure, and the journey toward shedding those extra pounds is often fraught with challenges and hurdles. From dieting to exercising, from buying bigger clothes to spending a fortune on them, the process can be long and arduous. But with patience, support, and encouragement, the couple can navigate this shared woe and emerge on the other side with a greater appreciation for each other and a stronger bond.

CHAPTER 16

WHO IS NOT PREPARED FOR THE "EVENT"

Woe is a word that has been around for a long time. It appears over 100 times in the Bible. Some of the many definitions of the word are: "misery, suffering, trouble, pain, disaster, depression, distress, grief, agony, gloom, sadness, hardship, sorrow, anguish, misfortune, unhappiness, heartache, heartbreak, adversity, dejection, wretchedness".

However, there can be additional circumstances that a husband or boyfriend can experience with their significant other that go along with the above. Open communication can resolve some of these conflicts—others take a more subtle yet intense form.

One such example is what I call "the look," which is a piercing, hard glare that conveys much of the above, and the man now understands that something is amiss and more we will follow. Another tactic employed by some women is the silent treatment which can last for days on end. It is a powerful tool that can create loneliness and leave the man wondering what he did wrong and when it will ever end.

Then there are insidious tactics— like maneuvers that seem innocent enough but put a man in a vulnerable position. Some could be called external, involving the transferring or sharing of woe. It should be noted that most of the woe incurred by a man is what would be called self-inflicted, where even a small misstep can lead to monumental amounts of woe. This episode will address a shared woe.

Today's epistle is one of the woes that a man must endure when he is faced with those awful words of a scheduled EVENT (wedding, banquet, company dinner, dance, etc.)—anything that might suggest something more formal to wear than jeans and a tee shirt. As I perused the invitation before me, I couldn't help but feel a sense of dread. It was a formal affair, and while I knew I could handle it, I also knew that my dear wife would be put in a state of major woe.

Those last few words of the last sentence should give you a clue as to where this is heading. Men, by our genetic nature, just look at these events as another thing where we might have to get on our good suit and maybe a tie and wear socks. Women, on the other hand, look at this as a major catastrophe in the making, even if it is approached with great forethought and planning and involves the husband, especially when he really doesn't want to be involved.

The first words out of the wife's mouth are," I don't have a thing to wear." Actually, woe has entered the wife's life in her mind at this point, regardless of how nice the event may be. Many of the meanings of woe listed above have now settled into her body. However, the point of this article is not to focus on her woes because, as we husbands know all too well—the wife's woes are now the husband's woes, and what is he going to do about it?

The first thing a husband should never do (and this is with painful experience) is to say, "you've got all sorts of nice things to wear." The mere mention of an extensive wardrobe is enough to trigger a chain reaction of despair and frustration, culminating in the infamous "look" —a glare so intense it could melt steel.

I braced myself for what was to come—a litany of reasons why none of her beautiful clothes were suitable for the occasion at hand. No matter how logical my suggestions were, they fell on deaf ears. In her mind, there was no outfit in her closet that could satisfy the complex set of expectations and standards she had constructed for herself.

Each passing moment brought her closer to a state of utter panic. Even the fact that it was the event she had attended before—say, the annual company dinner a year ago—there was no way she would wear the same nice dress. Women have much longer memories than men regarding who wore what a year ago. She would have to have something else. In a sense of desperation, my wife declared that there was only one option left—shopping. And, of course, this presented many challenges.

As we ventured out into the crowed stores and boutiques in town in search of that elusive perfect outfit, it was a journey fraught with frustration and disappointment, with issues of finding the right one in the right size and color. It was a daunting task, made all the more challenging by the time crunch—the event was a mere month away.

Eventually, something was found, but it would have to be altered and sent to the cleaners to be pressed. Finding someone to do the alterations with a time crunch was never an easy task, but it was accomplished. And, of course, the husband would have to take the clothes for alterations and cleaning and retrieve them.

Any EVENT that presents itself in your life is going to cost you money. The husband often will have to take his wife shopping which increases the woe the husband has even more. Another thing a husband should never do is look at the price tag of whatever she hands you to hold. Do not even think about saying, "wow, this is how much?". This will get you "the look," followed by many other choice words. Remember, the object of trying to reduce your woes is to reduce her woes, even if it may take a bank loan to pay for it.

Beware of the woe that may present itself—your wife, when she gets charged up with all the shopping, will now think it will be necessary for you to get some new clothes. Always try to plan on not having to walk through the men's section or, better, go to a women's store. Fortunately, they are so focused on what they think they need that this is sometimes an afterthought, and you need to be ready with reasons why you have to get home or anywhere quickly, and what you have in your closet will look just fine.

As time marches forward, the pages of life turn and the stories we create unfold before our very eyes. Efforts are made, events are had, and memories are etched into the fabric of our existence. Though some may fade with time, others will stand the test and bring us joy for years to come.

In the realm of companionship, a simple compliment can go a long way. When your beloved dons a new outfit, take a moment to let her know that she looks radiant, for such words can uplift even the weariest of hearts. And yet, as you glance towards her side of the closet, perhaps it is best to avert your gaze. For within those depths lie countless items, bought with good intentions, but destined to gather dust for eternity. A sight best left unseen, for it may bring about a twinge of melancholy for both you and your partner.

The moral of today's woe is that when an EVENT comes along, you will not be able to avoid woe. The relief or overcoming the woes experienced should be all that you need (other than paying for them).

Conclusion

By now one can see that a man in a marriage can expect to see a variety of woes. He needs to be prepared because they can come as a result of his own actions or lack thereof, by the sharing or transferring from his wife, necessary ones, and inevitable ones.

All of the woes noted in this book were based on actual experiences of the author and all except one (Barking Dog) involved his wife. Most all of the woes were experienced during the first half of the marriage—The Event and Weight Gain ones were ongoing.

There was a maturing of life here that made the author more aware of what he should do and to be a little more ready to deal with the unexpected. Perhaps this book will have enlightened the men (and women) about woe. The Boy Scout Motto "Be Prepared" would be the best advice there is.